I AM ~ THEREFORE I THINK

MARI BIRO

Photo of Mari Biro   1980

I AM ~ THEREFORE I THINK

Mari Biro

Man is only a memory in his own mind

and in the minds of others~

Mari Biro

For Julian, Michael and Diana

Dark Self Portrait   pencil on paper 2014   Mari Biro

BEING

Ignorance, or lack of knowledge regarding the existence of life beyond this planet is limiting the Self to a constricted and rather primitive view of the Universe.

Thus, the Universe consists solely of the Self's awareness of the Self and the experiences of the Self that occur in a small area of the planet's surface during the state of existence of the Self's Being.

The Self is not able to escape consciousness of itself, nor is it able to grasp that the same exact phenomenon is taking place in every other Self on Earth.

All this is causing a permanent state of insanity and a perpetual state of confusion for the Self.

The sense of guilt emerges when the Self is incapable of feeling and experiencing the pain and the pleasure of another's Self. The Self does not understand that it is not responsible for this, that the limiting existence of the Self is simply an inevitable condition, one beyond its control.

Perhaps there is a reason for its Being, the Self speculates on occasion. The Self is alone. It is a tragic Self and a lonely Self. The Self struggles to escape captivity from an invisible cell of self-awareness and the knowledge of this awareness. The Self's cell walls of self-awareness are impenetrable. The Self itself cannot break through these walls except inward. There is no way out.

The Self maintains the same identity till awareness of itself ends.

The Self's identity changes only in the event of illness or injury (schizophrenia, amnesia following an accident or trauma, split or multiple personality disorder).

Unbearable pain and anguish render the Self no longer capable of survival while having awareness of itself. Consequently, a change of identity takes place in the Self in order to save the Self from NONBEING.

ON THE KNOWLEDGE OF THE OCCURRENCE OF DEATH

The feeling of DREAD

Knowledge of the inevitable occurrence of Death coexists with the fear of the absolute annihilation of the Self, the Total cessation of Being.

Being goes through a brief cycle of life during which the Self negates the death of its own Being. The knowledge of the Self's future death, threatens to destroy the quality of all the moments of its existence while it is alive. Thus, the knowledge is feared, abhorred, negated, forced into the deepest recesses of human consciousness. It remains lodged in there throughout the duration of the Self's Being.

Existential Diversions   pencil on paper   1995   Mari Biro

The knowledge prompts the Self to drown itself into a safe sea of diversions. This sea is filled with mental and physical acts designed to cause the Self temporary loss of memory of that knowledge through repeated intervals of time.

Why such fear, why such dread of Death? Why such denial? While existing in a state of Being, the Self assumes an extraordinary sense of self significance. A burden of huge magnitude, this sense of Self's sense of uniqueness and irreplaceability becomes a major reason for the angst that begins at the onset of conscious thought and ends at the time of the Death of such thought.

Terror of the Death of Being is so consuming that the Self is willing to trade Death for the prolonged physical and spiritual suffering in the event of illness or injury.

Then there is the terror of the 'Terror' ..
Avoidance of any thought over the inconceivable thought of NON-BEING is the only path for escape from a life of unbearable turmoil.

On DEATH

The Self is trapped inside the cell of its own consciousness. It is incarcerated and condemned to awareness of its own Being, as well as the knowledge of the finitude of its Being.

The possibility of life after Death can fill the Self with a terrible sense of dread at the thought of life being eternal.

A terrifying thought, an eternal trap for a self-aware Self. Is this a choice any Self would want to consider? What is not known is extremely frightening and the Self is terrified of the eternal. Paradoxically, the Self does not want the game to be over. On the other hand, it does not want the game to last forever.

ON THE NATURE of MAN'S EVIL

Man is good and man is Evil as it is judged by man. How does man judge his acts to be Evil? Man's ability to think enables him to think of thinking, speaking and committing evil deeds against living things. The reason for this is that man has been programmed to live a life of self-awareness. His state of self-awareness is understood by him to be his connection to his own conscience. Being aware that his Being is aware of his Self, man knows that he is Being, thinking and acting. Therefore, he knows he is responsible for his own deeds that take place with his knowledge of them.

Where does the urge to be Evil come from? Man's knowledge of his own mortality fills him with a terrible sense of dread that he cannot escape from as long as he is conscious and self-aware. The question of what his purpose is for Being recurs incessantly throughout his life-cycle. Why strive to do any of the things that he fills his time with?

The sense of futility regarding all the work and all the motions he goes through during his existence on Earth consumes him. The conflict between his belief in a purpose and his belief in the futility of his actions creates an ongoing neurosis in man, holding him hostage in a life-long prison for the doomed.

The reason for his failure to commit suicide is his childlike sense of curiosity of what lies ahead and his terror of the unknown, due to his ignorance of the world beyond his world of Being.

Rage for coming into a type of existence in which he is doomed from the beginning, a type of existence that has his own Death looming over his head destroys him. There is one thing he knows, one thing he is certain of… Death will take him away from Life and no one can save him, not even GOD.

How does man survive a life that is filled with the knowledge of his own dreaded Destiny? He doesn't. That is, he wouldn't survive unless he would live in a permanent state of sedation. He self-medicates with numerous acts and ideas that fill up the ocean of his delusions which he crosses over from the port of Birth to the port of Death.

While on the cursed Titanic, he dances, he drinks, he gorges on food, he indulges in vices, he plans, he dreams, he suffers with pain, and hopes that the captain will keep the ship afloat a while longer, so this wonderful and painful journey will not end, not just yet..

Man doesn't want the journey to end, but he knows it will end. This makes him angry, it enrages him, he feels betrayed, violated and he becomes thirsty for revenge. Revenge on whom? There is no clear target to aim at, so man turns on himself. His evil acts are directed against others of his kind as well as himself, so he can vent his fury at the ineffable, invisible Enemy in a Universe that forced him into a state of Being that must absolutely End.

Man is taking out his rage on living things because nonliving things would greet him with absolute Indifference.

The victim's intense reactions make him feel alive. Their death makes him feel omnipotent. When he brings death to a living thing, he becomes God, or god's equal. Thus, he becomes God's rival, or the Invisible, Omnipotent power's powerful Enemy. This helps him face his own Death, look Death in the eye without fear or dread. He repeats his evil acts when he realizes that he cannot keep up a race with the Invisible force that controls his destiny. With or without a conscience, his deeds make him vulnerable and so he continues his desperate battle with the demons of Death.

The man who copes with the Knowledge will refrain from inflicting Evil onto others.

The man who is unable to cope will inflict Evil onto himself and others.

My Eye   pencil on paper   2003   Mari Biro

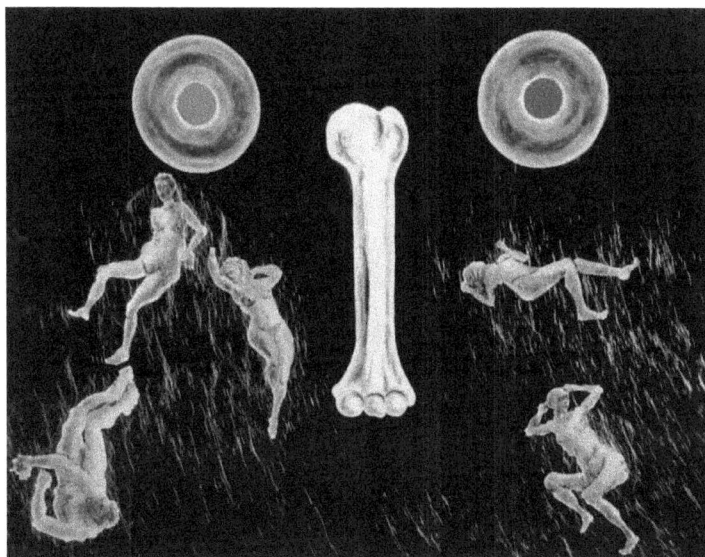

I – detail   oil on canvas   2014   Mari Biro

I

I see only my I

You see only your I

My I is trapped until it escapes

The consciousness of my Self

Your I is trapped until it escapes

The consciousness of your Self

My I and your I will **never** meet

I – detail   oil on canvas   2014   Mari Biro

How can I be so convinced of being I

When you are so equally convinced of being I?

I -detail   oil on canvas   2014   Marı Bıro

Your] sees your] in the mirror of my] on this panel

My] sees my] in the mirror of my] on this panel

If we both look in the mirror

My] will meet the image of your] and

Your] will meet the image of my]

I   oil on canvas   2014   Mari Biro

My I will have a concept of what your I

Is to your Self

But my I will not fuse with your I

Your I will have a concept

Of what my I is to my Self

But your I will not fuse with my I

I – detail   oil on canvas   2014   Mari Biro

My | will see the |mage of your |

My | will know it is the image of your |

I – detail   oil on canvas   2014   Mari Biro

My I and your I are separately trapped

In the web of our separated consciousness

I – detail   oil on canvas   2014   Mari Biro

The panel your I is looking at demonstrates

That the Self of any I

Is not able to escape consciousness of itself,

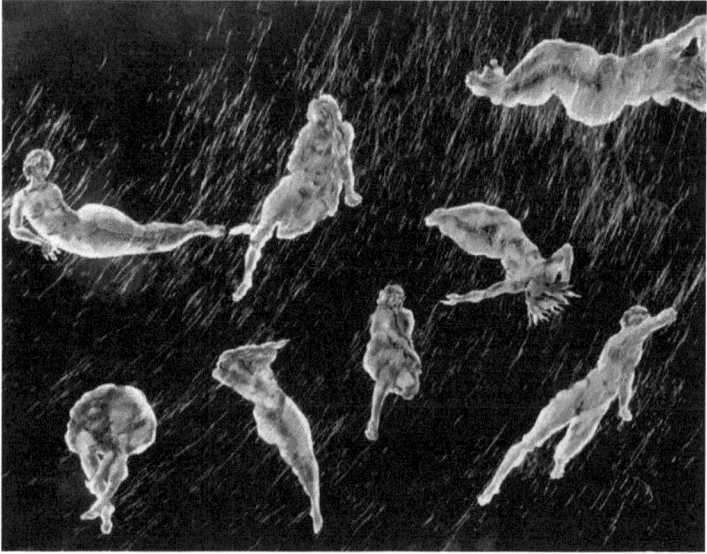

I – detail   oil on canvas   2014   Mari Biro

Nor is it able to grasp

That the same exact state of Being

Exists in every other Self on this planet

You know what the shiny circular things are

You know **nothing** about the labyrinth

How 'it' was created

I – detail   oil on canvas   2014   Mari Biro

Trapped in the labyrinth

The shells of the Selves

Are praying for the suffering

To end

One shell is mine

APHORISMS

Existence   ~ an absence of definition

Art   ~ the poetic protest against evil

Life   ~ the hopeless orbiting of personal

                     experiences around one's trapped

                     conscience

                   ~an avalanche of questions,

                     always the same ones that fall

                     into the Death Ravine without

                     answers

                   ~ a star, upon which the human

                     passerby coming

                     from nothingness, halts to rest

                     for an instant in order

                     to continue his journey into

                     further nothingness

Consciousness   ~ a mysterious and isolated

                     phenomenon

Perspective	~ a linear illusion
Philosophy	~ a whirlpool of questions sucked into the depth of Eternity
	~ a malady of intensified self-awareness
	~ a state of suspension between total lucidity and insanity
Insanity	~ a state of Being involved in the active pursuit of self-imposed diversions (masochism)
Dreams	~ unconscious researches for definition
Love	~ the absence of Evil

Self-reflections   pencil on paper 2003   Mari Biro

THOUGHTS

Thoughts~ I lost many of them~ they will never reenter
the same way~ I'm a different person as if a new Self
had replaced my old one~ actually, not really, the

old one is there, it's always been there, since I acquired awareness of it, since I've been capable of thinking~

This awful Self, a self-aware Self, stalking my body, stalking my brain~ so powerful that it drives me insane, as it does my fellow humans~

Sure, it gives me breaks, generous pauses, deceptive ones aimed at fooling me into feeling free of it~ they are the diversions, myriads of them~ they work, they make me forget about the Self, the Self that belongs to my *I*, the one that exists immaterially inside my consciousness~ it is like GOD~ I cannot see it, feel it, touch it, hear it ~ I can only be aware of it in a maddening way..

What has happened to me? To my I? To my Self?

Who are these living creatures around me? They are humans like me~ we all share the same destiny~ we will all perish in various ways~ at various times.. None of us know ahead of time.. unless ill.. We do not know one another.. Yet we all share the knowledge that one day we will cease to exist…

This is a train~ a subway~ driven by another human's 'I'.. Around me, others, humans who share my destiny..

They are taking a break now.. they are immersed in diversions~ chatting, reading, staring at their cell phones..

Now on the platform ~ a human I, singing.. It transports him and us away from our Selves..

My Self has changed~ it has actually changed its perspective on the world~ on life.. It's been gradually moving away from the Insignificant which is closely related to experiences that have created a life of memories relating solely to my own specific identity. It has moved over to the Significant~ the unfathomable Universe~ that which encompasses all living and dead matter…….

From infinitely small to infinitely vast…….

One becomes immeasurably more philosophical when aging and after the loss of someone one had been intensely connected to..

It seems I'm not one of them any more..

These humanoids around me… I ask them in my mind, do you know? Do they not know that the 'reality' they cling to might not exist? Do they not wonder about who they are? Where they come from? Are they not as scared as I am?

In the grand scheme of things nothing matters…
Everything just is.. We are all part of it, part of the
grand scheme… We are all dreaming a dream…

Perhaps we share the same Self and we do not know it..
we are all phantoms..

I see us five hundred years in the future and I see the
present through the eyes of those who lived 500 years
ago .. I see the past of 500 years ago ..

I see them looking at us who exist in the twenty first
century.. I am in it, in the 21st century.. I am the future
that you from my past never got to see..

They float around me.. They are the phantoms of a past,
same as I..   I see them 500 years from
now in 2516.. I see them now.. I freeze this image for the
future.. They are the phantoms of the future.. We are the
phantoms of the future, phantoms of the year 2016.. The
year 2016, 500 years in the past of the year 2516...

I see them both.. I experience the past as I experience the
future.. Both inside my mind containing the present Self
of my Being..

Thought – four and a half decades ago

There is a mode of thinking in which the elimination of the essence of a wish obscures this essence through the forced imposing of some nonexistent negative factors, that grow, persist and pour poison over the returning road. Slowly, the effort to penetrate deeper, disappears.

***

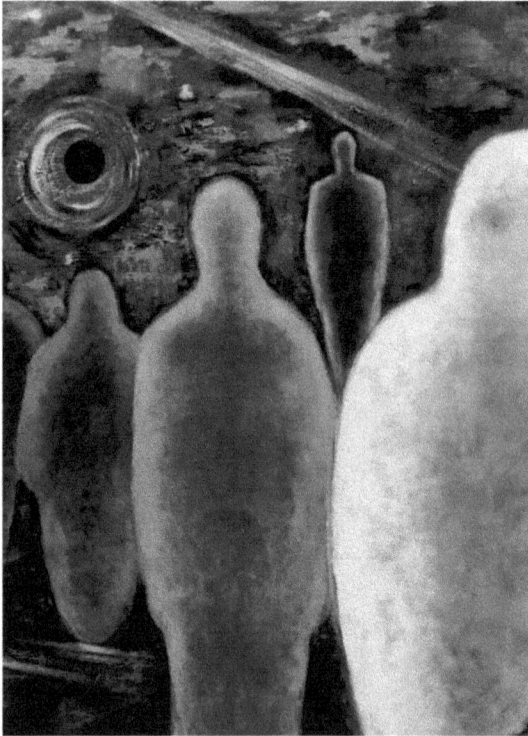

Dark Matter   oil on canvas   2016   Mari Biro

I see the phantoms around me now and I am amazed that I know the future.. I exist in the year 2516, in 'their' future..

I freeze these phantoms in time, now, for the future, knowing we shall not exist then~ 'they' of the future will not see what I see now..   I have Power.. I can see us from the past and I can see us from the future..

Nothing we see, hear, smell, touch, know, matters, except to our own Self, the Self, providing us with infinite imagination created through the experiences of our Selves, leaving a trail of memories....

The silence in my mind when I'm alone with my Self.. The distracting noise when I leave my Self temporarily..

Awareness and Self-awareness~ two different planes of existing....

Why have we humanoids been programmed to cling to life? Why are we desperately fighting for self-preservation? Why do we want to escape our fate, that of the total cessation of our existence? Why have we been given brains and consciousness? Why??????????????????????????

The extraordinary power of the mind.. the human mind.. Time.. Relativity.. their connection to the mind .. Perception .. the mind's ability to alter it completely... a process that begins at the onset of a shocking event, or following deep trauma.. If existence seemed partially surreal before, it becomes entirely surreal after... one exists in an altered reality, in a parallel universe.. Which one of these realities is correct? We shall never know because our mind constructs, deconstructs and transforms everything we perceive, or imagine we perceive... To be of a philosophical mind is to accept that our existence might be imaginary, that anything we strive to achieve, or accomplish, borders on the threshold of absurdity. We are self-imagined phenomena, playing self-imagined roles in the theater of the absurd. Tortured souls till Death brings relief through our release from the captivity we all cling to.

We know of It, we know we all know of it... we are all perennially restless while burying the feeling of dread into our subconscious...

We have all been punished to suffer ceaseless torment...

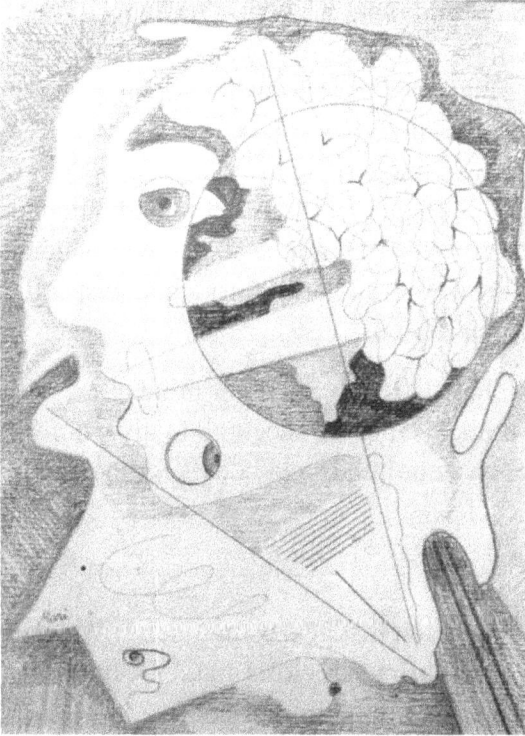

Periphery of Thought   pencil on paper   2014   Mari Biro

Even if we sink into a philosophical state, carried to the extreme periphery of thought, where we become too terrified to be able to function as before, even then we are pulled back to the state of 'before', the one we are comfortable and familiar with. This happens because we have been programmed from conception to exist in a zone of limitations regarding thought~ a zone with a safety net around it that insures our survival…. We cannot bear to fully comprehend and accept our fate… we cannot bear to be reminded of it every moment…it would mean we would not be able to complete the cycle of life we were born to orbit throughout a specified time period for each of us…

We tremble with terror when our mind allows the entry of such thoughts, but we succumb to diversions because they preserve our minds and bodies for the duration of our life cycle…

Thus, a revelation that gets us in touch with our cosmic consciousness brings us closer to GOD, the GOD we all fear whether we are faithful or not.

That instant gone and we return to being mere mortals… our consciousness reduced to that of helpless earthlings.. Our mind expands and contracts till it wears out and leaves our planet altogether to join the eternal forces of the Universe.

To meet Einstein.. To listen to his passionate words on the mystery of Time, space travel, the flow of light…

Why has there only been one Leonardo Da Vinci? Only one Michelangelo?

One Mozart? And all the other unique, great minds?

What enables some minds over others to be more capable of pondering at the deepest level?

The Self metamorphoses throughout the aging process. The more advanced in years, the closer the Self draws to the Universe. The Self gains the capacity to comprehend that *It* too is being prepared to depart the planet where it has existed in a shell that is completing its life cycle. The Self becomes more and more focused on the role it's been playing through its ephemeral existence on the home planet.

The Self begins to realize that it must leave on its own eternal journey to the outer limits of a Universe that is shrouded in an Eternally unsolvable mystery.

While in its stages of childhood, adolescence and youth, the Self is unable to comprehend what lies ahead. The concept of mortality on the home planet is dwarfed and replaced by the dominant concept of Immortality in order to enable it to complete its life cycle and fulfill its destiny on Earth.

The phenomenon of aging, the advancement in years, will give birth to a *new* type of philosopher.

Thus, shall begin the speculations and torment that shall cease when the Self departs~ or so the human hopes……

ON MAN'S DEHUMANIZATION

Man's acts of self-dehumanization and self-alienation are gradually causing him to suffer the total loss of his sense of identity. As he self-incarcerates in an age of rapidly advancing technology, he is driven to search for ways to get in touch with his inner self in an increasingly futile attempt to save what is left of his soul.

Psychoanalysis has been taking place in the public arena, with modern theories circulating and infiltrating the minds of large numbers of cult followers who are seeking refuge from the threat of an imminent apocalypse.

The birth of the Robot has become the milestone for the new social order.

Yet, man is trying to save himself and society from the imminent death of the spirit. Tragically, he is slowly suffocating inside the structures he has built where the walls are closing in on him in a prison that is getting more and more confining around him. Man tries to stay human, divulging his inner secrets to the stranger who does the same from the isolation of his own cell.

ON IMMORTALITY

Immortality means ad infinitum... Ad infinitum means endless time. . . Time is endless in cosmos.
Man is suspended in cosmos (space) attached to a planet through the force of its gravity, prisoner in a bubble of oxygen (the global atmosphere). Man cannot escape this bubble that robs him of his immortality. while his essence is locked up in a fleshy cage.

Man's essence stays locked up in a fleshy cage. Man lives and dies with the notion that he will cease to exist. His dreams suggest to him clues to his immortality. But all this happens in chaos, and since man's brain is not fully in use, it cannot comprehend such information. The dream tells man that time is relative. Man can dream of a past event and relive it in all its authenticity as if there was no lapse of time since the event had occurred. A 60-year old woman dreams she is 17 years old now and she has no conscious awareness that 43 years had passed and she is in fact 60. The woman dreams of a personal experience and the dream is a personal dream simply because the woman has a particular identity on earth that she is familiar with. Her earthly identity (reflected through her self-awareness) and her timeless essence meet with timelessness in the dream, where she is given the message of her immortality.

If Universe is infinite and timeless, man who is part of the Universe is also timeless, or eternal. As we know, the human brain is only partially in use. What about the other part? Is there less chaotic information in there? Which recesses of it are dream creators? Why are dreams inevitably haunting us?

There is something that desperately tries to reach us through the dream, perhaps the locked recesses of the human brain are trying to communicate to us information. I once read something on the feeling of immortality in youth. It would be interesting to point out that though man is doomed to suffer in his condition, he has the capacity to experience the feeling of his own immortality for a while. This while or time period happens specifically from birth to a certain point in his early youth.

Here I note that while the material layers surrounding man's essence are fresh and young (in Earth terminology), 'that' which guides his thought, experiences a conceptual feeling of his own immortality.

There is of course, the dim awareness of the inevitable end of his existence, but that is an extremely alien dream like concept. Man's home in Cosmos has agonizing proof of the Truth of the fall and death of man.

We only know the concept of death from an earthling's point of view. We were of course never told how the rest of the Universe views death.

Getting back to my previous point, man is closer to the feeling of his immortality while young. After a certain point in his youth, the feeling fades and man continues his existence without it. Instead of his former attitude toward time (a phenomenon he used to take for granted) man begins to hurry and prepare for his mortality, a fact of life that approaches him the older he gets, the faster. Man's adaptation to the knowledge of his own end ensures his own survival and it takes place simply because he is not given another Choice.

Does this mean that man is closer to his true essence in his youth which feels eternal, only to move away from his essence as he gets older? When his outer layers finally experience total deterioration and cease to function, his true essence is freed. It flees into the Universe escaping the bubble of oxygen. It flees into Vastness and Timelessness, where it has no Earthly identity any longer. It blends into Cosmic Totality existing throughout Eternity.
Or perhaps it travels to another captor. That is to be endlessly speculated on.

www.ingramcontent.com/pod-product-compliance
Lightning Source LLC
Chambersburg PA
CBHW071436040426
42445CB00012BA/1379